Grand Harbour Malta

Grand Harbour Malta

Photographs by Kurt Arrigo

MIRANDA PUBLISHERS

Published by **Miranda Publishers**
139/3 Tower Road
Sliema, Malta
www.mirandabooks.com

First edition 2011

Designed by Mark Thomson Studio
Printed in Italy

ISBN 978–99909–85–45–0

Special thanks to the following for their invaluable assistance:

Dr Timmy Gambin (Consultant Editor)
Dr Albert Ganado
Dr Stephen C Spiteri
Lino Bugeja
Joseph Muscat

Endpapers:
front: Textured details of a warehouse door illustrate the erosion brought about by time.
back: The classic sailing yacht 'Barney' on a starboard tack approaches Valletta from a north-westerly direction.

pp. 2–3:
Waves batter the fortifications, offering a spectacle unrivalled in the Mediterranean.

Contents

Harbours

Timmy Gambin

The sea was, and indeed still is, essential for human existence. For centuries people, goods, ideas and ideologies have travelled, spread and arrived by sea. As a provider of sustenance, the sea was believed to be boundless. It is only recently that humanity has started to treat the marine environment as the precious, delicate and finite resource that it is. If the sea provides the invisible tracks – ever-moving and changing routes determined by varying winds and currents – then harbours can be likened to stations, places where journeys start and come to an end. For millennia, harbours have been deemed of utmost importance. The ancient Greeks had numerous words that referred to the use of coastal spaces by ships and mariners. In English too one finds multiple references including harbour, port, anchorage and haven.

As much as ships are made to be guided across expanses of open sea, they must ultimately make contact with land where they can take on or discharge cargo – whether material goods or human travellers. Some harbours evolved into focal points for specialized trade. In antiquity, the large man-made ports of Claudius and Trajan just north of Ostia in Italy were built to accommodate the thousands of ships that carried just about everything necessary for Rome's existence. Smaller harbours often tended to be more versatile, catering for the transfer of goods, pilgrims and docking of naval vessels. Today, many ports and harbours have evolved to cater for specialized cargo such as containers, or for different maritime activity such as yachting.

Through accidents of geography and geology, Malta was primed to play an integral and significant role in the history of the Mediterranean. The geographical accident referred to is Malta's location, which however is not unique in the central Mediterranean. There do exist other islands in similar geographical locations, namely Lampedusa and Pantelleria. Together with Malta and Gozo, these islands are located at the narrowest stretch of the Mediterranean Sea. The often repeated yet unavoidable cliché is that the central Mediterranean islands have been at the crossroads of history and culture. However, if this is the case, why then is the history of Lampedusa and Pantelleria so sparse when compared to that of Malta and Gozo? The answer to this can be found in the aforementioned 'accident of geology'.

The Maltese archipelago, with Malta in particular, is rising at one end and subsiding at the other, at a rate that is not perceptible to its inhabitants. This long-term geological phenomenon existed long before Malta was an island, when it formed part of a large land mass protruding southwards out of Sicily. Such a phenomenon determines the islands' drainage – rain falling on the area that was to become Malta was pulled downwards by gravity to a massive river that flowed across a vast plain, which is today located underwater somewhere in the Malta-Sicily Channel. Millennia of heavy rainfall and severe flash floods cut a series of deep river valleys which still form an integral part of the Maltese landscape and are known locally as *widien*. Through these *widien* the 'geological accident' extends from the land into the sea. Following the end of the last ice age some 15,000 years ago, sea levels rose and gradually filled Malta's river valleys, turning them into the fjord-like inlets which may be observed today. Well, not quite! Scientific studies have proved that in ancient times, Malta's harbours, such as those at Marsa, Burmarrad and Marsascala, extended further inland and were significantly larger than they are today. The inner reaches of these harbours acted as receptacles for the tons of sediment carried down by flood waters and which have been consistently carried through the valleys and deposited downstream. Thus, inner-harbour areas gradually evolved from a marine environment to one that was lacustrine and eventually into a dry floodplain.

Over the past centuries, this evolution of Malta's harbours has had a bearing on how these spaces were utilized, perceived and settled. Of all the harbours in Malta and Gozo the Grand Harbour is the largest. It is formed by a series of river valleys that provide drainage for the largest catchment area of fresh water. In some places, the main river valley which is today deep below the main channel of the Grand Harbour is over 60 metres deep when measured from sea level to bedrock. The sea is also generally deep, which means that the harbour has been able to accommodate the ever-increasing size of ships brought about by technological advances in shipbuilding. There can be little doubt that the Grand Harbour is the most important harbour complex in Malta as well as in the central Mediterranean. This is true not just because of its size, rivalled in the Mediterranean only by Port Mahon, but also for the variety of shelter offered and numerous access points to the hinterland. It is the Grand Harbour that distinguishes Malta and its history from its central Mediterranean neighbours.

The history of the Grand Harbour is both long and varied – people, land and sea all intertwined into its rich historical fabric.

Harbour of Worship

Ever since humans ventured out to sea they have linked maritime spaces to realms of spirits, gods and goddesses. For the ancient Greeks and Romans it was Poseidon and Neptune that dictated the ferocity of winds and much-feared storms. As safe havens where journeys commenced and if one was lucky, ended, harbours were often marked with temples and shrines. During the third millennium BC, the inhabitants of Malta and Gozo undertook the construction of numerous megalithic temples throughout the islands' landscape. On a promontory overlooking the Grand Harbour, no less than three such temples were built – dominating the maritime landscape below. Harbour sanctuaries in the area are not limited to the prehistoric period. In the nineteenth century, dredgers working in the vicinity of Marsa brought up a number of marble columns and the torso of a Roman statue. These remains have been linked to a Roman harbour temple in the Grand Harbour. This ancient synergy between harbour and deity is not dissimilar to that which may be observed at Marsaxlokk where the temple of Juno at Tas-Silġ dominated the bay below. The affinity between mariners and the divine knows no cultural and chronological barriers. Christian believers in the Middle Ages would have been able to observe landmarks in the form of the churches of Saint Lawrence in Birgu and that dedicated to Saint George in Marsa.

Places of spiritual significance were not necessarily marked by buildings. The intangible nature of such spaces and related rituals make them difficult to pinpoint. Clues may be deduced from place names which give a discreet insight into the perception of a particular area. St Elmo's Point, located at the harbour mouth, provides one such clue. St Elmo is one of the patron saints of sailors and there can be little doubt that the point of entry to the harbour was witness to unrecorded rituals dedicated to this saint. In later times, the tip of the headland opposite St Elmo's obtained notoriety for a reason that was not spiritual but is intriguing nonetheless. Gallows Point assumed its name from the corpses left hanging there by the Knights of St John so as to leave newly-arrived travellers in no doubt as to the severity of the law on the islands.

Ritual and pageant are still very much part of the Grand Harbour's heritage. In the recent past, thousands of small craft sailed out to meet the large catamaran that was carrying Pope John Paul II. This flotilla followed the papal craft in an improvised maritime procession.

Harbour of War

Malta, with its geographical location and large harbours, was a place worth fighting for. From its harbours attacks could be launched, supplies delivered and shelter offered to warships. Furthermore, the harbour was often seen as a distinct domain – a part of the island that looked seaward rather than towards the hinterland. In 218 BC, at the dawn of the second epic struggle between the Carthaginians and Romans, the latter determined it necessary to conquer

Malta. This action, led by Titus Sempronius, removed an advanced Carthaginian naval base. The 2000 soldiers left to defend the island points to the importance attributed by the Carthaginians to their offshore outpost with its precious harbours.

Struggles for control of and access to the Grand Harbour persisted through time. In 1283, one of the largest naval battles was fought just off the 'Castle by the Sea', today known as Fort St Angelo. Angevin and Aragonese fleets battled in the large basin just below where the Bighi Naval Hospital currently stands. What is of note here is not who was victorious (for record's sake it was the Aragonese) but rather that two leading Mediterranean powers were willing to fight and lose ships for possession of the harbour and its castle.

The importance of the Grand Harbour was not lost on the Knights of St John when they took possession of the islands in 1530. Upon their arrival, the Knights took it upon themselves to strengthen the existing defences around the harbour area as well as constructing new fortifications. Such activity attracted the attention of the Ottomans, eternal enemies of the Hospitaller Order. Following a series of small raids on the islands the Ottomans finally launched an armada which carried an army bent on expelling the Knights from Malta. The islands' harbours had become a hive of maritime activity with Christian ships sailing from Malta to attack Ottoman shipping as well as that of their allies. During the Great Siege of 1565, the besieged were trapped between rock and water. The sea provided a protective barrier which, despite determined efforts, the enemy failed to cross. In a seaborne attack launched from Marsa the Ottomans sent hundreds of their elite troops on small boats. Men and craft met their end after receiving heavy fire from a concealed gun battery. Eyewitness accounts describe other gruesome events that took place during the siege. One in particular remains inextricably linked to this brutal conflict. Following the capture of Fort St Elmo, the Ottomans crucified some of the defenders and sent their bodies floating across the harbour towards Fort St Angelo. The severity of the siege propelled the Knights of St John into an obsessive flurry of fortress building – a costly obsession that persisted well after the real threat of a second siege had long since faded.

It was not for another 150 years after the departure of the Knights that their fortifications would receive a battering from weapons against which no common walls could withstand. Just like the Ottomans in the sixteenth century, Axis forces in the last world war could not bear the havoc wreaked upon its shipping, havoc that in part originated from ships and submarines based in Malta's harbours. Flying out of bases in Sicily, the aerial onslaught of the enemy was both audacious and relentless. Bombs weighing half a ton brought fortresses, churches and houses crashing down. One daring attack was launched from the sea. Human torpedoes and explosive boats attempted to infiltrate the harbour defences. An unplanned explosion near the breakwater alerted the Maltese gunners led by the legendary Colonel H. Ferro. Shots from Fort Ricasoli and Fort St Elmo repelled the attack, which became known in Italy as the 'Glorious Failure'.

Today, the seabed bears witness to the battles fought over Malta in World War II. Shipwrecks, parts of planes and other wartime debris can be found in various parts of the harbour. It is not uncommon for unexploded ordnance to be occasionally dredged up from the deep. Within its sediments, the Grand Harbour must hold well-preserved secrets that may one day shed light on slivers of history such as the doomed Ottoman attack in 1565.

Harbour of Exchange

Where there is a harbour one will find commerce. What differs from one harbour to another is the level of commerce. Factors influencing levels of commercial exchange can be both internal and external and both are not mutually exclusive. Islanders, by their very nature, learn to live with historical undulations. Oscillations between times of plenty and leaner periods become a de facto way of life often dictated by political and economic decisions taken elsewhere. As an island, Malta has been the receptor of both negative and positive influences from overseas.

An advent of plague, such as that which entered Malta from Alexandria in 1813, could blacklist the islands' harbours and cause an economic depression. This incident followed a blockade of Italian harbours in Napoleonic times which had turned Malta into a hub of entrepot trade, with the Grand Harbour assuming the role previously held by its unfortunate competitors. War too brought about mixed fortunes. In the mid-nineteenth century, the Crimean War brought unprecedented growth to Malta's economy, which however went into serious decline at the end of the conflict.

One must not only look at Malta's recent past for examples of how the Grand Harbour was used as a centre for exchange and redistribution. When ancient Rome depended on grain shipments from Egypt, Malta and its harbours was moulded into a satellite port. The island fitted into the grander scheme of things and thus formed part of Rome's *façade maritime*. Large warehouses known as *horrea* were constructed in the Marsa area. These were used to store grain in optimal conditions whilst the transport ships, such as that used by St Paul to depart from

Malta, wintered in the harbour. These storage facilities may have been the first built around the Grand Harbour but they were certainly not the last. Grand Master Pinto da Fonseca financed and built an elaborate warehouse complex complete with quay and church. Other storage facilities were developed over the past two centuries, some by official decree, others by individual entrepreneurs.

It was not always exchange that propelled economic activity. Technology too contributed to the commercial interests in the Grand Harbour area. The advent of steam engines turned Malta into a vital coaling station where ships could stop to take on fuel and other vital supplies. Many local shipping companies, some still operating today, can trace their roots back to this period. Likewise, the opening of the Suez Canal in 1869 redirected shipping lanes from the African route to the Mediterranean. Ships sailing between Britain and the Far East were redirected through the Mediterranean, making Malta an ideal staging post. Throughout history, market forces overseas also dictated what local produce was shipped out of the harbour. Medieval ships loaded with locally grown cotton sailed as far afield as Spain, a practice that continued well into the eighteenth century and possibly later. It was cheaper cloth from India that eventually rang the death knell for the production and export of Maltese cotton.

One cannot separate the petty and mundane activities from the 'bigger picture'. Where there are people conducting big business one may find others offering a variety of services on the periphery. In the Grand Harbour, money passed through a multitude of hands. Boatmen, beggars, fishmongers, prostitutes, tradesmen and hawkers could all be found in large numbers at strategic locations around their harbour and its cities. All, except perhaps the beggar, provided a service in exchange for cash. These masses of individuals provided the smaller cogs in the works that drove the harbour and its economic activity.

Harbour as Destination

Today, the Grand Harbour is still witness to a remarkable degree of economic activity. Recent technological innovations such as the development of transport containers have caused the migration of some cargo handling away to other harbours. However, new activities have evolved and maritime spaces have been reinvented and adapted. In Dockyard Creek, a once industrial and naval zone, one finds a modern yacht marina which provides a completely new chapter of maritime use for the Creek. Therefore, industrial areas are being converted into recreational spaces with the historical fabric maintained for more contemporary uses. Pinto Stores, left in partial ruin

for decades, have been restored and now receive the modern sea-traveller arriving on the modern behemoths of the sea – cruise liners. The old water taxis are making a comeback as opportunities arise. Thousands of people are taken through the Grand Harbour every year on small harbour cruises, which despite their brevity give a unique and unforgettable glimpse of the harbour and its grandeur that is perceptible only to those who view it from the sea.

The Grand Harbour is so much more than can be expressed in words. Through the images presented in this book the viewer will be transported into a place that has been shaped by time, but that has in turn also shaped history. This visual exploration should not end with the last page of the book. On the contrary, this book will hopefully inspire its viewer to look at the Grand Harbour with new eyes and to appreciate it for the gem that it really is.

overleaf: A spectacular aerial view of the Grand Harbour. One may note the various peninsulas that make up this natural harbour complex.

11

'A documentary of a place in my lifetime'

Kurt Arrigo in conversation with
Mark Thomson

Mark Thomson: We have often talked about how the history of a place is written into its architecture. What is your experience of change in the Grand Harbour?
Kurt Arrigo: A harbour is by nature a place of movement and transition. For centuries civilisations have inhabited the port, and consequently it was natural for the topography to evolve and change with the times. After the Second World War, the area fell into decline, and the docks became less central to our lives. However in recent years there has been a resurgence of interest in the harbour area and restoration of many of the buildings is taking place. So far the integrity of the Grand Harbour has been maintained, and I hope the future changes planned for the embellishment of the harbour continue to be positive.

What do you think of the marina now?
The marina represents the next phase of the harbour's maritime use, it is a low impact project that is contributing to the regeneration of the harbour and its surroundings.

In your previous books there has been a lot of underwater photography, but there's none in this one. Why is that?
It's not easy to capture underwater life in the harbour because the water is murky and visibility is poor. There are some areas where you're not even allowed to dive because of the shipping traffic. So instead I chose to explore the harbour above sea level.

How deep is the harbour?
It would probably draw at least 20–25 metres, and then in the main harbour it descends to 25–30 metres, gauging from the size of ships that enter the port.

It's such an important place in Maltese and European history, the sea bed must hold many stories.
What lies on the sea bed of the Grand Harbour is a big mystery. Unfortunately it hasn't been feasible to do a proper excavation. You would probably have to stop sea traffic and it could potentially be quite dangerous. I remember my father diving outside the breakwater and pulling up a live bomb. Back in 2002 I went diving with Timmy Gambin who was involved an archaeological survey linked to the Grand Harbour Marina. The amount of pottery that lies on the seabed, beneath the silt is, well, another story.

So you would pass the Grand Harbour on the way to school?
Yes, as a child I vividly remember one of the biggest tankers coming into the Grand Harbour; we were in assembly and suddenly told to go and have a look at the biggest tanker coming into the Grand Harbour. I think it was in Dock 6, the biggest dry dock that was built by

the Chinese, and only recently completed. However my fascination with the Grand Harbour started about 15 years ago when I began to feel the need to try to capture its uniqueness.

One of the things that's very interesting about the work and the book is that you haven't just looked at the 'big-hit' moments – the side of Fort St Angelo, the glamorous parts, – you've really gone into the dark side of the Grand Harbour, up around Marsa, in the underground tunnels and other places that are rarely visited or explored.
I think it was really important to dig deep into the soul of the Grand Harbour, be it the oubliette in Fort St Angelo or the rawness of Marsa. There's also some awesome architecture down there, from the time of the British. Later with modernisation a power station had to be built and for many years the Marsa power station was a big polluter and eyesore.

One of the most powerful images in the book is of the ships' graveyard in Marsa, with the rusting submarine and clouds reflected in the water.
The graveyard is perhaps the most telling part of the harbour, and though the ships come here 'to die' they remain a vital part of the cycle of life in the harbour. The movement of the clouds in the water serve to remind us of the continuity and inevitability of change, which is where the elusiveness of beauty so often lies.

There are a lot of clouds in the book, and there's a lot of drama in there as well. It's somehow a very big story.
I always felt that the name, the Grand Harbour, merited drama and impact. I felt that there had to be contrast within the elements of nature, whether lingering on the calm, or being overwhelmed by the pounding seas, brewing storms or sheets of rain. Life in the harbour is about shelter from the elements and is a stage for the battle between man and nature.

Weather plays a very big part in Malta anyway, as a small island surrounded by a large water mass...
Absolutely, you're always being battered from one side, whether it's a north-westerly or a north-easterly or a southerly wind. I found it better to shoot in the winter months when the light is warmer and less blinding than it is in the summer months.

Let's talk about Fort Ricasoli; from the land side it is not particularly visible and quite difficult to get to. But once you do, it's a beautiful piece of architecture, imposing and dramatic.
Fort Ricasoli is disintegrating; which is a tremendous pity as the architecture is absolutely phenomenal, with the

interior built by the British. A few walls have been restored, but the work is not nearly enough. The enormous space, which you can see in the aerial shots, has been used as a set for quite a number of epic films – and in fact that is what the fort is currently being used for. Whether it will ever be restored to its full glory, I don't know, but it would surely require great investment.

How did you get access to Fort St Angelo?
There are two ways, the top part is accessed through the permission of Fra Critien, the resident Knight at Fort St Angelo. He was kind enough to allow me to photograph it. The lower part falls under the patronage of Heritage Malta. There is currently a restoration project going on there and they allowed me access. They also helped me photograph the inside of the oubliette.

Is the oubliette open to the public?
Currently you are not allowed to walk in there because it is considered to be dangerous. There is a strong feeling of claustrophobia in there. It's very small inside, and to think that prisoners were kept down there – all they could do was engrave the walls to pass the time, because they certainly couldn't walk around and get any exercise.

Caravaggio was supposed to have been imprisoned there.
I don't think we can really confirm whether he was actually put in the oubliette, or whether he was allowed to roam freely within the confines of St Angelo.

There are some interesting buildings along the side of Dock One but I've only ever known them as ruins.
What's interesting is that the lower part was built by the knights, then the British built the upper floor. So if you look at one of the images you'll be able to notice the varied architectural styles. Most stunning is the sophistication of the engineering of Dock One.

There's a strong contrast between the cavernous deep-perspective images and the extreme close-up details – the numerals, the sign painting on some of the store-cupboard walls, as well as some of the historical graffiti.
There is so much to learn from the details of what is left behind; all imprints of the lives that have passed through here. The mason's mark, the fortifications, or the graffiti down below Valletta are all ways of people talking about the Grand Harbour of their time – there are the inscriptions in the oubliette, the mason's marks in the stone, the 'logo' in Marsa, and below Valletta, the paintings of submarines and ships.
    Another place is the boom defence where there is a wall full of old pictures of warships coming into the Grand Harbour. The present owner doesn't do much more than

fish here, yet the history is still there, on the walls.

Hard to photograph but fascinating are the still visible damages from the war in some of the walls, especially just below the mortar bell.

You have also taken many aerial photographs of the Grand Harbour. Here the relationships to the early maps and imagined aerial perspectives becomes very clear.
When you think of how they actually did it, creating imaginary perspectives, it's quite amazing. It's also a fascinating place from the air, especially Valletta with its modern grid pattern. In fact, Birgu was also built with architectural precision but it's less visible now because it was heavily bombed during the Second World War, and when it was rebuilt the city lost some of the grid lines.

There is also an interesting relationship to the well known Second World War reconnaissance photos of bomb damage to the docks – when you consider how much bombing that little area was subjected to it's amazing that so much of it is still there at all.
With such a concentration of ships that were in the harbour during the war years, it took quite a drubbing, and many lives were lost. Yet the harbour continues to give testament to the complex history of the Mediterranean Sea, from the sixteenth century up to the present day. We are fortunate to be able to continue to live within the bastions and cities built with such architectural expertise.

One of the interesting things about the harbour is the layering of history there; events seem to be laid one on top of the other.
It is a natural harbour because of the way Malta slopes on the easterly side, and thus the sea continuously flows into the harbour. The story starts from everything being thrown, or pushed into the harbour, and then the layers have piled up to create the myriad references we see today. The Grand Harbour is being used for various activities, one of which is the start of the prestigious Rolex Middle Sea Race, a 606-mile yacht race that starts in Malta, circumnavigates Sicily and its archipelago and ends back in our waters. To see the harbour bustling with spectators along the bastions and some of the world's finest sailing vessels is spectacular.

There are sections in the book on the Easter parade and on the regattas, traditional parts of Maltese culture.
There are two regattas held each year, both with intense rivalry between the harbour towns. There's a lot of local pride at stake, and they fight it out in a rowing battle on the water. The harbour is really brought back to life on these two days and again, the intimacy of the inhabitants atop of the walls and along the water's edge is a sight to behold. Religious feasts, namely Good Friday and Easter Sunday, are days of solemn devotion and baroque splendour. The cities around the harbour, in particular, boast processions and statues that have a long historical and uninterrupted standing.

You have been going out at dawn to shoot, whether it's by the breakwater or on the pilot boat – obviously part of capturing the drama is being there at the right time?
The early hours of the day on the harbour are magical. The day rolls in as the pilot boats navigate out to greet the enormous ships entering port. I asked if I could join them a few times, and was privileged enough to travel out with them early in the morning and experience a true sense of a working life in the harbour.

I began to return to certain spots over and over again until I felt satisfied. I've been shooting the Grand Harbour over the past eight years, and I would say I have been down to the breakwater at least 50 times, so it became a meditative process.

Much of the harbour is changing now, and some of it is going to be lost, isn't it?
Some of the details may well be lost, and certainly some of the decadent beauty. The British built the dock, which is a masterpiece of architecture. On the dock walls there are various depth markings, roman numerals and Arabic numerals that indicate the water levels. To take those photographs I was hoisted up by one of the immense cranes and lowered onto a platform, in order to get close enough to shoot a detail on a wall. I also climbed down into the Dock 6 to position myself below the bow of a huge tanker. In the Second World War the British had built an underground tunnel for their operations, and there's also a lot there that is photographically very interesting but quite challenging to capture. I feel it is really important to capture this nautical heritage whilst it is still there.

I look at Dock One now, in a state of transition and modernisation, and I am glad I have captured it in its raw state. The minute you start putting tables and chairs in front of a place you create another screen in front of it. In the shots that I managed to capture a few years ago, you can still appreciate and imagine the harbour in a former time.

The emptiness of some of the images is laden with history; almost written into the fabric of the harbour.
There's so much material that could be put into a museum, but will it ever happen? Will somebody see that and be able to appreciate it? I know the dry docks have an enormous amount of equipment that would have been used in World War II, for example. The Maritime Museum is the largest museum in Malta, but I don't imagine it could ever house all the relics and artefacts to be found in this area.

In a way history has caught up with the Maritime Museum now, because what was the contemporary view is also now history; the viewpoint from which that museum was created has now become a historical one.

One does begin to question these things. That's why it was really interesting to hear what the various consultants in this book, all renowned experts in their field, had to say. [The historical experts, Dr Timmy Gambin, Dr Albert Ganado, Stephen Spiteri, Lino Bugeja and Joseph Muscat were involved in the process of captioning this book, by showing them the photographs and inviting them to talk freely about what they saw.]

What are you shooting with?

I started off shooting with film on medium format transparencies and then made the transition to digital, high-resolution images. I've used five different cameras as they've evolved from one year to the next. None of the images have been manipulated – the images are honest and truthful. I wanted to capture the many stories that have unfolded here, which are the dramatic and wondrous stories of Malta.

In a way it's a documentary of a place, isn't it?

Exactly. It's really a documentation of a place in my lifetime.

p. 19
Scheme for the fortification of Mount Sceberras

This priceless manuscript map provides the solution to the creative genesis of the city of Valletta. It is the first project for the founding of a city fortress on Mount Sceberras. The illustration shows the original drawing made by Bartolomeo Genga (1518-1558) a highly esteemed military engineer in the service of the Duke of Urbino. He died in Malta on the 7 July 1558 soon after he submitted his scheme to Grand Master Jean de Valette and his proposal fell through. The fortress city is shown cut off from Fort St Elmo built in 1552 and the land front is in line with Corradino Heights on the east side of the Harbour. Only one copy of Genga's map is extant.

Maps from the Albert Ganado collection

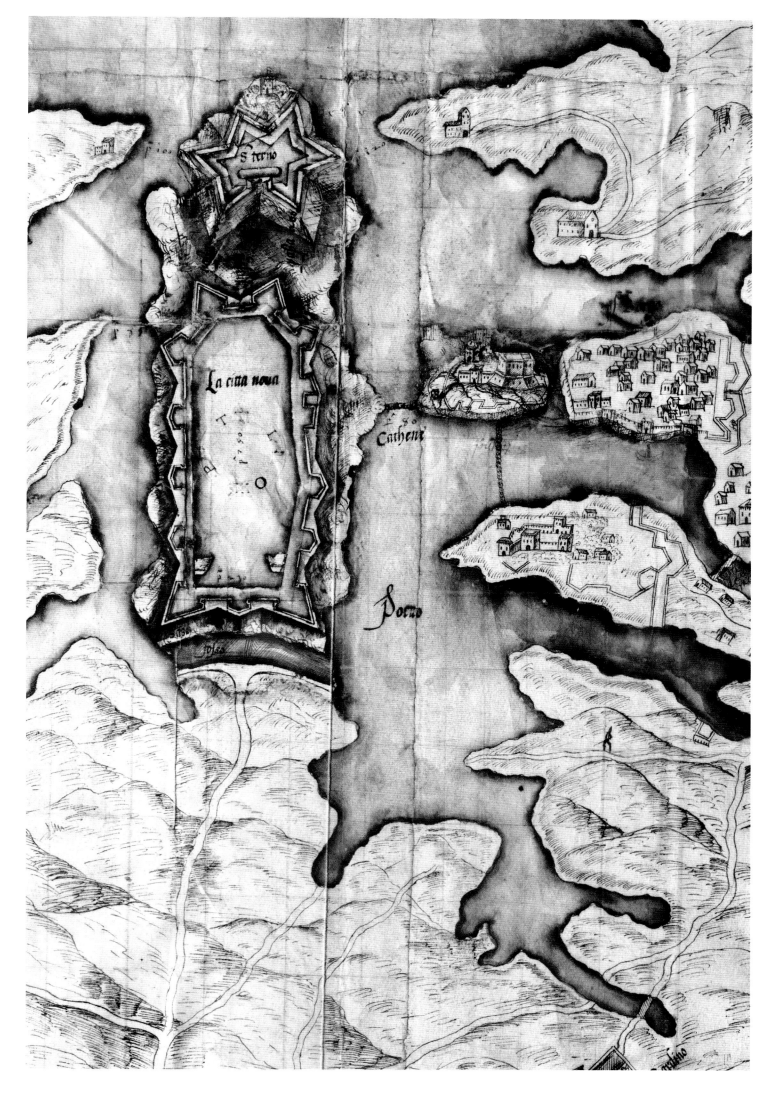

S ʒ rno

La citta noua

Catheni

Porto

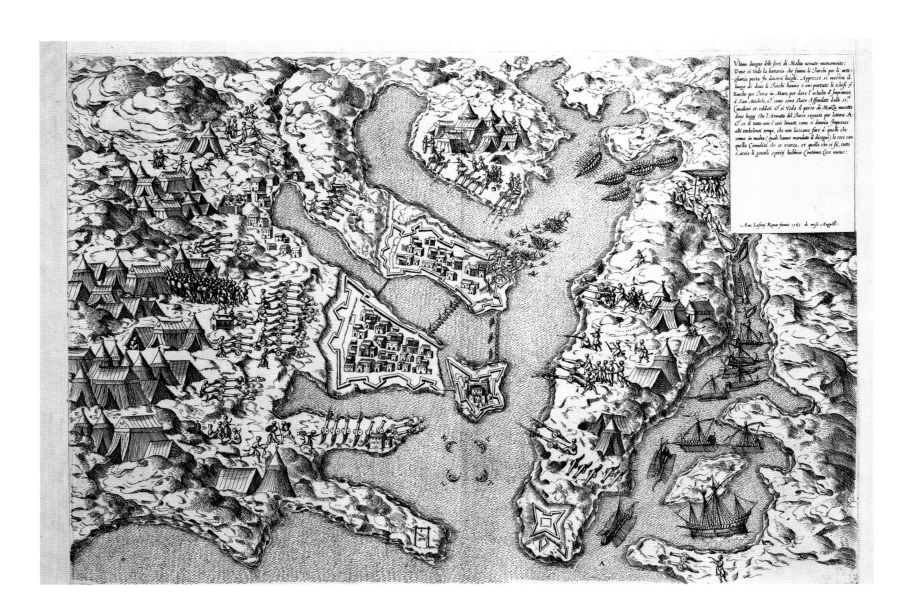

A Siege Map of Valletta , August 1565

In the sixteenth century, no newspapers
existed and illiteracy was widespread. But
people still wanted to be kept informed of
events at home and abroad. Enterprising map
sellers like Antonio Lafreri rose to meet this
demand, publishing 'news maps' which
illustrated important events in a manner that
the general populace could easily follow. These
were incredibly popular, and the most in
demand of all were the series of maps depicting
the Siege of Malta by the Turks in 1565.
Sketches were sent from the scene to be
published in Rome. In 1565, over fifty such
siege maps were distributed, showing the
progress of the siege and the eventual retreat of
the Turks. There might be five maps published
in a month, which would be sent all over
Europe and pinned to church doors, enlighten-
ing the illiterate masses and encouraging
donations.

This map shows that St Elmo has fallen and
Turkish troops surround the beleaguered
Maltese populace, who are hemmed into Birgu
and Senglea. In the top right corner we can see
ships which the Turks had transported
overland, and an attack on Senglea from the
rear is taking place. We can also see the bridge
which linked the two districts during the siege,
and two chains strung across the inner harbour
to prevent the Turkish ships gaining access.

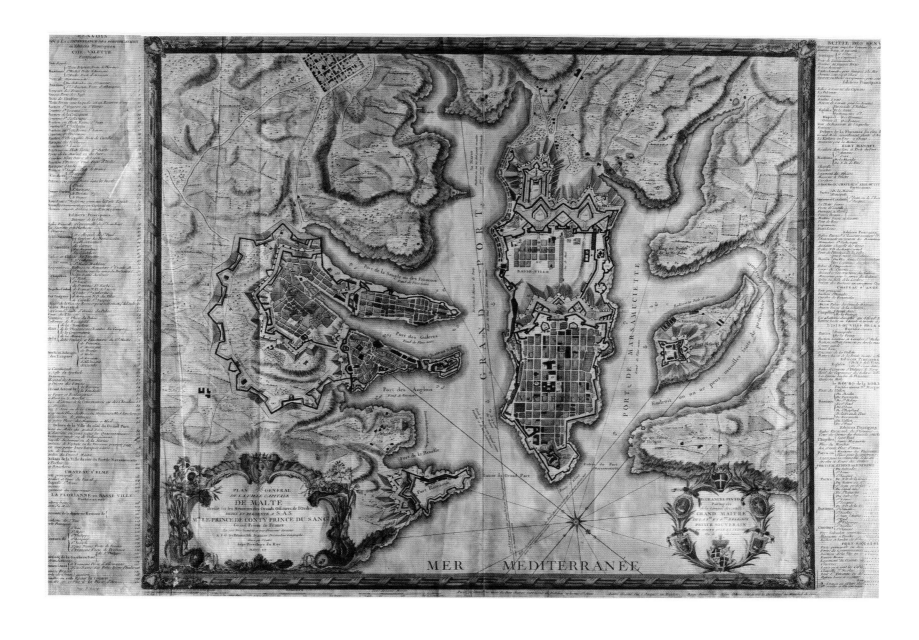

Valletta, c. 1751

This is possibly the first map of Valletta showing plans drawn up by the French engineer, geographer and publisher A.F. Gervais de Palmeus. It is one of the most colourful maps of the Grand Harbour in existence, in spite of the fact that it was published in black and white. For special clients, in this case the Grand Master of Malta, maps would be hand-coloured in the studio.

This map shows how the harbour had been fortified since the siege of Malta. Fortifications were deemed necessary to stop enemy fleets disembarking en masse and to strengthen the defences of the citadel to repel any approaching forces. The Commissioners of Fortifications and War constantly made the development of fortifications a priority over all other projects like town planning. The fear was that a force like the Turks would return and the settlement would not survive this time.

Grand Master Nicolas Cotoner was responsible for many of the improved fortifications including Fort Ricasoli (on the bottom left of the map), and the Cottonera fortifications, which can be seen in the middle of the picture. This plan of 1751 was re-issued in 1757.

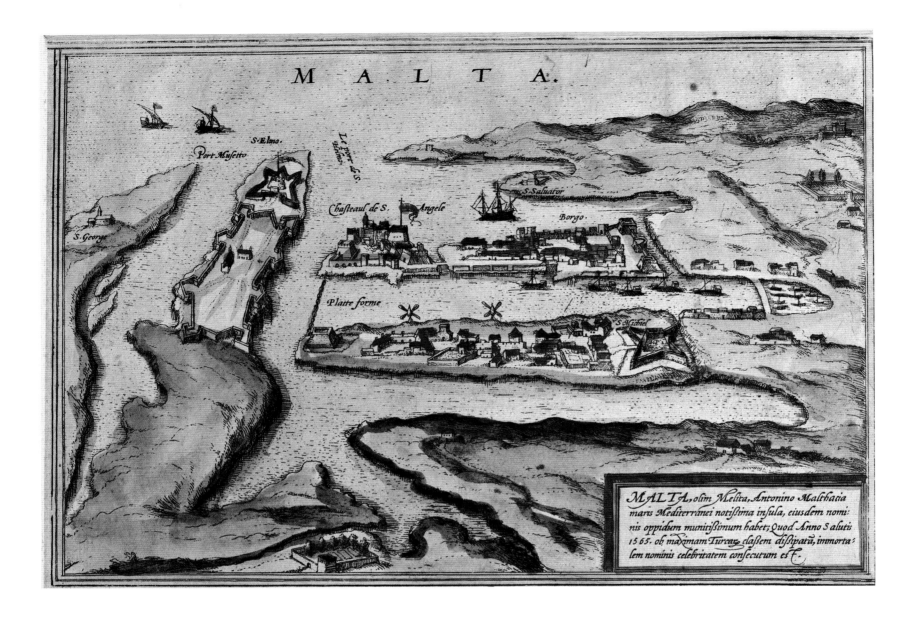

MALTA.

MALTA, olim Melita, Antonino Malthatia maris Mediterranei notiſſima inſula, eiuſdem nomi: nis oppidum munitiſſimum habet; Quod Anno Salutis 1565. ob maximam Turcar. claſſem diſſipatã, immorta: lem nominis celebritatem conſecutum eſt.

Map of Valletta and the Grand Harbour, 1572, Braun & Hogenberg (detail)

This map was published in 1572 in the first volume of Braun and Hogenberg's famous *Civitates Orbis Terrarum* – Cities of the World. *Civitates Orbis Terrarum* is considered to be one of the first true atlases, containing 546 views of world cities by the time the sixth and final volume appeared in 1617. It was a commercial proposition, intended for armchair travellers the world over, and each engraving was accompanied by a description of the city's history and businesses.

This Malta map was one of four maps which appeared together on a single page. It shows a

plan of the harbour which had been drawn up by Italian architect Baldassare Lanci, who had been brought to Malta by the Grand Master in 1562 to draw up plans for the fortification of Mount Sceberras. This was to be the site of the Order's new city because of its natural defences. Today, of course, this is where Valletta is sited.

This map was out of date by the time it was published, as it shows a plan which was drawn up in 1562 but abandoned by de Valette in favour of the Laparelli plan, which forms the basis of modern day Valletta.

The map shows a chain which was laid across the inner part of the harbour between Birgu and Senglea. When the Turks laid siege to Malta, the Grand Master saw that closing the mouth of the harbour would be impossible but once St Elmo had fallen, Birgu and Senglea were the only areas which needed defending. The chain prevented the Turks entering the inner harbour and protected the galleys of the Order of St John. A bridge was also built over the harbour to allow the traffic of weapons and troops between the two districts.

Bird's-eye view from inside the harbour, 1804

This bird's-eye view is from the Marsa and Cospicua side of the harbour. It was published in 'The History of the Order of St John' (1804) by Louis de Boisgelin. These 'bird's-eye view' maps were compiled from sketches drawn from several vantage points, but without the aid of trigonometry, and they are a testament to the capabilities and imagination of the artist.

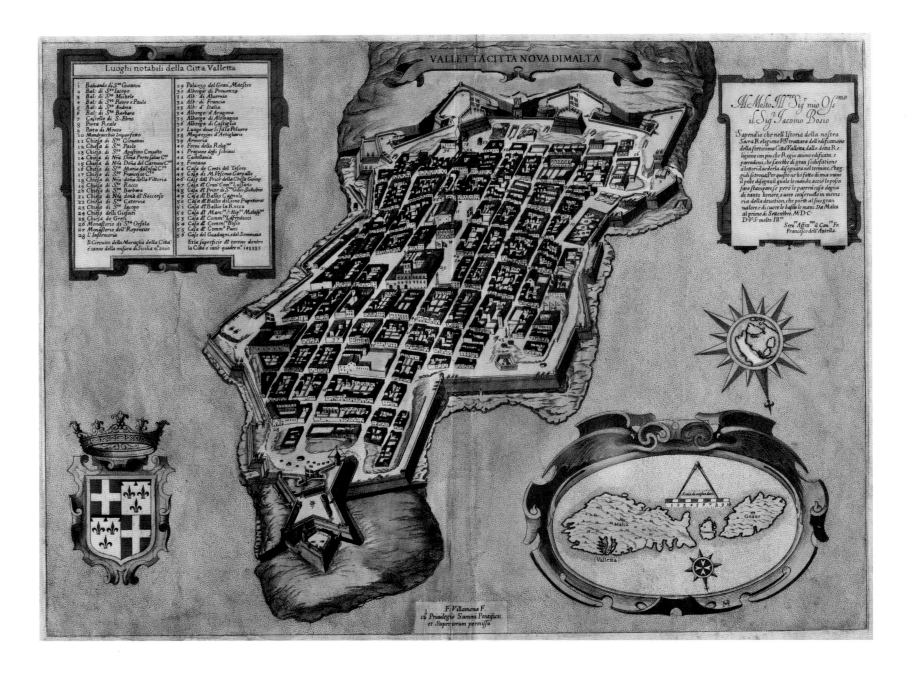

Street plan of Valletta, 1602

Italian architect Francesco Laparelli was commissioned by Grand Master Jean de Valette to draw up plans for the building of a new city with stronger defences following the Great Siege of 1565. Laparelli drew four plans of the city, outlining the street plan in the third and fourth engravings. The Knights of the Order moved to the site, on the Sceberras peninsula, in 1571 and construction of the new city, which became Valletta, went on for decades. This map is an engraving by Francesco Villamena from a copy of a manuscript map made by Francesco dell'Antella and published in Giacomo Bosio's 'History of the Order of St John' in 1602.

Valletta was the first city in Western Europe to be planned and built on a grid system. No one knows for sure what the inspiration for these plans were. Laparelli was forced by bad weather to take shelter in Sicily for three days while en route to Malta, and a popular theory is that he was inspired by the grid system he saw in towns like Carlentini. The refortification of Valletta continued until its surrender to French forces in 1798.

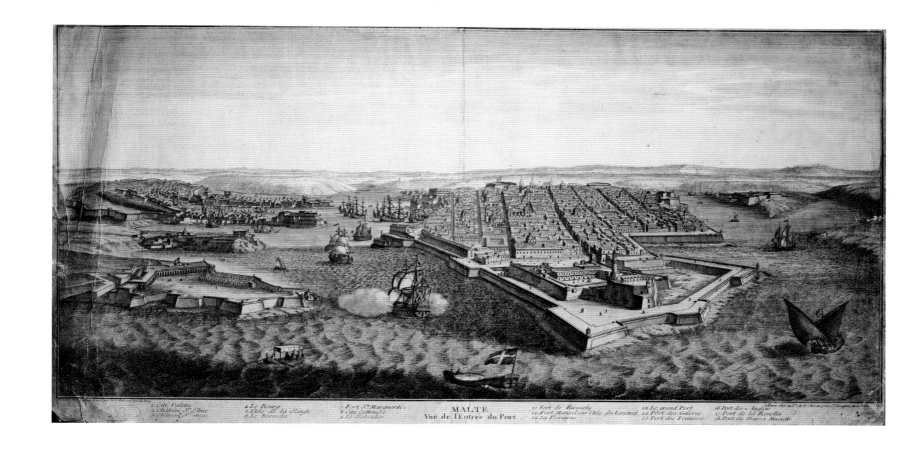

Bird's eye view of Valletta and the harbours

This view of the entrance to Valletta and its harbours taken from an imaginary point to the north was made by a French military engineer, Philippe-Nicholas Milcent. He came to Malta in 1715 and stayed for more than five years sketching the fortifications and panoramas of Malta. On his return to France, he engraved and published this view in Paris, together with another view showing Fort St Angelo, Senglea Point and the east side of Valletta. The harbour view was printed by E. Derochers. Both views were advertised in 1734 in the periodical *Mercure de France*.

The Grand Harbour has been used by mariners since ancient times, but the strong north-easterly winds, known as *gregale*, made it hazardous for ships to get in and out of the harbour. During the reign of the Order of the Knights, vessels had to seek shelter inside, and were often driven onto the rocks on the stretch of coastline between St Elmo and Valletta. It was not until British rule, in the nineteenth century, that the expertise became available to build a much-needed breakwater.

1 The Breakwater

The British decided in the 1870s that it would be advantageous to construct a breakwater to try to tame the violent north-easterly storms that buffeted the harbour, but they did not start surveying for another 25 years. Finally in 1897 a technical study was undertaken and the recommendation to build a shield was made.

There are in fact two breakwaters at the entrance to the Grand Harbour. The larger one, shown here, extends some 378 metres north-east from Fort St Elmo, and the other 122 metres from Fort Ricasoli. The foundation stone to the main breakwater was laid by King Edward VII on 20 April 1903 after the ceremony had been delayed by two days because of adverse weather. According to contemporary reports, the foundation stone has a brass casket within it containing local newspapers, coins, a sheet describing the running order of the ceremony and photographs of the Grand Harbour as it was.

The breakwater took more than six years to build. The materials were sourced locally as far as possible with the hardstone excavated from a quarry in Qala, on Gozo, the small sister island to the north-west.

The breakwater was a ground-breaking engineering feat involving the construction of foundation blocks of concrete weighing some 40 tons. These blocks had to be positioned and embedded on the seabed at depths ranging from 8 to 21 metres. It also required a labour force of over 1800 workers, including extra labourers shipped in from Sicily.

The breakwater cost more than £1 million to construct and was declared officially open in 1910. A recent survey of the structure confirmed its integrity for at least another 100 years.

Iron and the elements combine to produce
startlingly beautiful colours in unexpected
places. The bridge that once joined the
breakwater to the mainland is currently
being rebuilt.

2 Fort Ricasoli

Fort Ricasoli has played a crucial role in the military defence of Malta since its construction in the seventeenth century, never more so than in World War II when its twin six pounder guns were instrumental in overcoming the Italian E-Boat attack on July 26 1941.

The structure on top of the Bastion was the Fire Control Tower, from where troops would relay the coordinates of enemy vessels for the gunners to target and destroy.

The biggest threat faced today by Fort Ricasoli is erosion from the constant battering of the sea.

The combination of man-made structures, limestone rock, sea and sky creates a dramatic seascape at the entrance to the Grand Harbour.

previous pages: In recent years the Grand Harbour has hosted the start of the prestigious Rolex Middle Sea Race.

The breakwater is an almost inevitable extension of Fort Ricasoli, a combined defence against both the sea and enemy attacks.

Fort Ricasoli was designed by the Italian engineer Antonio Maurizio Valperga, as part of Grand Master Nicholas Cotoner's (1663–1680) plans for the strengthening of the Harbour's fortifications. This followed the scare induced by the fall of the Venetian fortress of Candia in Crete, the easternmost Christian outpost in the Mediterranean. The fort was named after the knight, Fra Giovanni Francesco Ricasoli, who generously subsidized the building costs.

52

These decorative spherical globes adorn the
top of Fort Ricasoli's entrance which, together
with Fort St Elmo on the opposite shore, has
guarded the entrance to the Grand Harbour
from naval attack for centuries.

Aside from its vital military function, Fort Ricasoli has more recently been used as a film set for a number of big budget Hollywood movies, including *Gladiator* (2000) and *Troy* (2004), where the compound was used to depict the exterior walls of the city of Troy.

More than 500 Maltese workers helped construct the sets and 1,200 extras featured in one scene of the film.

The stone walls of the fort form an extension
of the limestone cliffs on which it is built.

3 Kalkara

The British built an imposing hospital on top of the cliffs at Bighi (1830–1832), between Fort Ricasoli and the small village of Kalkara. This hospital treated thousands of navy personnel throughout Britain's rule.

The necessity of hygiene and general cleanliness was recognized in the British Navy early on. The natural baths they built close to the hospital though, while having the advantage of a continuous supply of water, had to be sturdily built to withstand the pounding they received from the storms that attacked the mouth of the Grand Harbour. Here the picture shows the effect of the erosion around the structure itself.

Interior of the baths. Despite years of neglect these historic structures still retain their architectural details.

4 The Three Cities

previous pages: The *dgħajsa* (pronounced dye-sah) is the traditional water taxi of Malta. It was the main means of transporting sailors from ship to shore and back again. The detail shown in the picture is the forestem – the front of the boat – which is shaped like a scimitar. There is also a balancing piece at the stern from which a lamp was suspended to make the boat visible on misty mornings or at night.

The oldest forestem pieces were made of teak and are used as a support for passengers climbing on to the boat. Interestingly on the racing *dgħajsa* (*dgħajsa tal-Midalji* – 'of the medals') they are detachable. The boatman stands up in the *dgħajsa* and uses two oars to propel the boat forward. British naval ships in the nineteenth century used to carry the *dgħajsa* as their preferred means of carrying sailors to shore throughout the Mediterranean and, on one famous occasion, a *dgħajsa* was lowered into the Grand Canal at Venice whereupon the boatman challenged a gondola to a race. To Malta's enduring pride, the *dgħajsa* won hands down.

Pilot boats in the Grand Harbour have been used since 1810. Before that the hulls of the ships were not deep enough to require safe passage into the harbour. In those early days, *dgħajjes* (pronounced dye-yes) were employed as pilot boats. Over the years the structure and materials of the *dgħajsa* were modified so that they could better withstand the severe weather that often battered the entrance to the harbour. Pilot launches – engine-powered boats – were not used in the Grand Harbour until after World War II.

Fort St Angelo dominates the inner reaches of the harbour from a military point of view, as this image suggests. When the Order of the Knights of St John arrived in Malta in 1530, they settled in Birgu and the first Grand Master of Malta, L'Isle Adam, made Fort St Angelo his home. The knights quickly realized the importance of the fort to the security of the harbour and the population, and set about fortifying it to withstand an unexpected Turkish assault.

They engaged the Italian architect Antonio Ferramolino to survey and suggest improvements to the Fort and the surrounding area. He designed a high cavalier, an imposing five-sided towering rampart, which rose above the original frontage. This allowed long-range guns to be positioned in defence of Birgu as well as the Grand Harbour, and was a crucial factor in withstanding Turkish assaults in the three months of the Great Siege of 1565.

The British recognized the military importance of the fort and in 1933 actually listed it as a ship – HMS St Angelo. In a curious quirk of history the Maltese government leased parts of the fort back to the Knights of the Order of St John, while other parts are currently undergoing restoration and development.

overleaf: Despite the severe bombing sustained by Birgu during World War II this aerial photograph highlights part of the ancient urban fabric of the city.

The Maritime Museum, housed in the former Naval Bakery, was built on the original site of the Birgu Galley Arsenal. This building was used for the construction and maintenance of the galley fleet belonging to the Order of St John. Three sheds were built over a period of thirty years until 1636, and the Order continued to improve this facility when funds were available. The arsenal survived until the end of the eighteenth century, and for three hundred years was a key element in the propagation of skilled labour and craftsmanship which allowed the Cottonera area of the Grand Harbour to flourish.

The marina at Birgu is a flourishing hub of yachting and boating activity.

overleaf: Cospicua, the scene of many a skirmish during the Great Siege of 1565. In World War II, this city and its brave inhabitants endured a battering from the air.

The solemnity of Holy Week is palatable in the atmosphere created during the rituals and processions that go back many centuries.

On Good Friday the guilds of the Three Cities carry statues through the streets of these historic walled towns. The carriers of the statues train all year round for the occasion and it shows in their exaggeratedly muscular shoulders! It is traditional for members of the public to carry the statues the last 100 metres to their destination.

When the traditional Easter celebrations were instigated, the influence of the Spanish was at its height and this is reflected in the costumes worn.

On Easter Sunday, in the Harbour area, a group of locals take over from the formal statue bearers and run uphill carrying the statue of the Risen Christ, to the applause of onlookers.

Fort St Angelo holds a pivotal place in Maltese military history as well as in the Grand Harbour, as shown by this view from the Upper Barrakka gardens in Valletta.

The history of the fort precedes that of Valletta and the Knights of the Order of St John. It was originally known as the '*Castrum Maris*' or 'castle by the sea'. It may have been used as a vantage point as far back as Roman times, and it was certainly in existence by the thirteenth century, when it was the prize in one of the largest medieval naval battles. On 8th July 1283, the Angevin and Aragonese fleets, fought each other for control of the castle and therefore, effectively, the harbour. The Aragonese won by blocking in the French fleet which was decimated when it tried to break through the Spanish lines.

From then on '*Castrum Maris*' ('Castle By the Sea') was under Spanish rule until the arrival of the Knights in 1530

The inside of the notorious *oubliette* (dungeon) in Fort St Angelo. A bell-shaped cell carved out of the rock of the fort which was probably a cistern before the Knights converted it into a dank, pitch-black dungeon. The oubliette (meaning 'forgotten' in French) had a covered opening at the top which was the only means of entrance and exit, and prisoners endured sentences of up to six months in these hellish conditions – freezing cold and damp in winter; scorching hot in summer. It was abandoned after the Knights reign ended and was only rediscovered in 1906 when the British Navy took over Fort St Angelo from the Army.

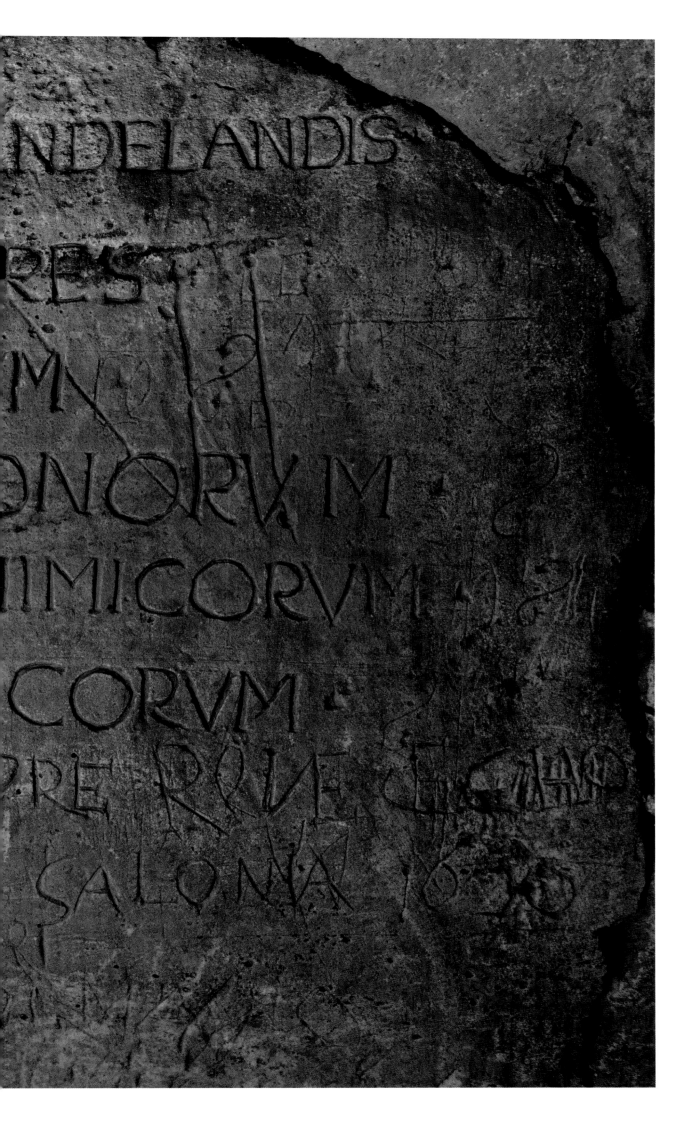

The quality of both the carving and the language of the graffiti on the walls of the oubliette reflects the education of the prisoners. These were normally sons of noble families who were either Knights of the Order or training to become one. Their crimes were generally related to duelling or brawling – most often over a woman. It is alleged that Caravaggio was incarcerated here for a fight of some sort.

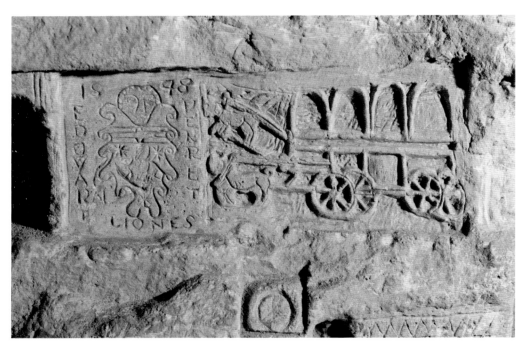

Details of carving in the oubliette.

Detail of the *Gardjola* at Fort St Angelo, one
of the many stone lookout posts that dot the
Grand Harbour.

The *Maċina* at Senglea was a lifting device for taking masts and rigging as well as other objects off a ship when it was coming in for repairs or for wintering. Originally the crane structure was constructed of wood but was subsequently replaced by a more modern metal structure. The evolution of modern cranes did away with this now obsolete facility, which was dismantled.

Senglea Point, the scene of one of the bloodiest
battles fought during the Great Siege of 1565.
Today it is one of the most popular vantage
points from where one can enjoy a view of
Valletta across the Grand Harbour.

Emotions run high during the regatta when inter-city rivalry is played out in front of thousands of locals and tourists alike.

Details of traditional racing boats that are used in the regattas of 8th September and 31st March. All these craft are painted in vivid colours that represent the various harbour towns. Athletes train year round in the Grand Harbour for these events and boats are meticulously cared for in the club houses.

The *Gardjola* at Senglea: this lookout tower is intriguing for a number of reasons. Its design and construction have been attributed to Evangelista Menga, who was an engineer working at the same time as Laparelli and was one of Cassar's teachers. The motif itself is of interest: each 'window' has a design mounted above it which symbolizes vigilance. Visible here are an eye, an ear and a hawk. The tower was dismantled before World War II so that anti-aircraft guns could be positioned there, but was subsequently rebuilt after the end of the war.

This picture shows a clamp mark on the side of a piece of stone used in the fortifications. The deep grooves carved into both sides of the stone enabled the arms of a crane to 'clamp' the sides and lift it without danger of it slipping. In addition to these, masons also made other marks – usually simple scratches in the surface of the stone – to show that they had carved it. Masons were paid by the quality and size of stone they carved and most were illiterate, so each had their own 'signature'.

There is a myth that the fortifications were all built by slaves. In fact most of the work was carried out by paid contractual labour, with the specialized tasks of quarrying and shaping the stone and ramparts entrusted to paid Maltese masons and craftsmen. To date some 96 different types of masons' marks have been identified on the walls and ramparts of the fortifications around the island. Slaves, when available in the winter season (for they were busy rowing the galleys in summer) were forced to undertake the unskilled jobs such as moving stones and carting debris.

overleaf: The Grand Harbour is a place of contrasts – those between old and modern; war and peace as well as between past and future.

previous pages: For those growing up around
the Grand Harbour, its waters have provided
a vital source of recreation: fishing, swimming
or simply enjoying the cool sea-breeze close
to the shore.

The Maltese Falcon: an extraordinary mix of
the historical and the ultra-modern, the
Maltese Falcon is one of a new generation of
sail/motor vessels that combine environmental
responsibility with unparalleled luxury.

A view of the new marina in Dockyard Creek looking out towards the Valletta landfront in the middle of the picture and Fort St Angelo to the right.

5 Dock One

Dock One, designed by British architect William Scamp and built in the first half of the nineteenth century, is shown here prior to the start of recent restoration works. The British extended the buildings on the right of the picture to include a ropery on the first floor.

Another view of Dock One looking west towards Dockyard Creek. Some of the buildings were used as stores for the squadron of sailing warships introduced by the Knights in the early eighteenth century.

A detail of nineteenth century Naval architecture which is commonplace throughout the Grand Harbour.

Some of the now-obsolete equipment in Dock One previously used to flood and empty the docks.

Textured details of signage within the
former Naval dockyard complex, showing
a water-level indicator (left) and other
miscellaneous signs (above).

The construction of the Grand Harbour Marina in Dockyard Creek has created a new maritime function for this historic area.

overleaf: The fortifications reflected in the water. No matter how many times one visits the Grand Harbour there is always something new to see. One can never be totally familiar with the place.

In the centre, high up on the fortifications is St Anne's Gate – the main entrance to Senglea, which was also called *Città Invicta* or the Undefeated City after the population withstood the Great Siege of 1565. (Birgu on the neighbouring peninsula was given the title *Città Vittoriosa* – the Victorious City.) To the right, the tower structure on the waterfront is the *Maċina*, a crane-like device which was an essential part of the working harbour.

6 The Drydocks

Pictured here is the Assembly Hall located between Docks Four and Five, which were constructed in the late 1800s when numerous ships were still being built in the harbour. During World War II, air raids by the Italian airforce forced many ship repairs in this area to go underground. The huge tunnels, which measure up to 100 metres, are to the left of the picture.

overleaf: A point of view with extraordinary perspective. For decades skilled workers ensured the completion of jobs on vessels of all sizes.

While the heyday of shipbuilding and repairs
in the creeks of the Grand Harbour might
be long over, there is still work to be done.
The recent privatisation of the Dockyard has
ensured the continued use of these drydocks.

overleaf: [pp. 144–5] Numerous workshops
were housed in the Assembly Hall. In the 1950s
the dockyard adapted from a military facility to
one more focused on commercial shipping.
[pp. 146–7] Cranes loom like silhouetted
giants. French Creek was once the hub of
maritime activity prior to the construction of
the naval dockyards in the latter half of the
nineteenth century.
[pp. 148–9] Detail of signs that dot the entire
dockyard complex.

7 Marsa

The harbour offers shelter to vessels of all sizes. Here one notes fishing trawlers moored under the bows of a large oil tanker.

URAGANO MFA 1002 LA VALLETTA

overleaf: In Roman times, a large port complex was established in the Marsa area, as it was set furthest back from the sea and afforded more shelter than the other parts of the harbour. ('Marsa' derives its name from the Arabic word for anchorage.)

Various parts of the Grand Harbour have played their part in modern films. The U-boat in this picture was used in the film *U571*, a wartime tale of the attempt to capture an Enigma decoding device from a German submarine (U571). The submarine has since been moored in an area of Marsa used as a ships' graveyard.

Ras Ħanżir, once the site of a grand Roman port, complete with quays, warehouses and a breakwater. The British developed this area into a commercial harbour in the 1860s. Local merchants established their businesses here after being uprooted from their base in French Creek. Disused potato sheds and rusting hulks adorn the waterfront.

The Galizia Arch and channel were built by the British as part of a process to drain the marshlands at Marsa to make way for the sports grounds which still stand on the site. Even now the channels serve an important function by draining storm water into the harbour and thereby preventing the whole area from flooding. The 'V' and 'R' on the bridge stand for Victoria Regina.

8 Valletta

previous pages: [pp. 160–63] The feast of St Paul's Shipwreck in Valletta commemorates the apostle's arrival in 60 AD. Street celebrations mark this event, which is held in February – outside the normal Summer festa season.

As with other towns around the Grand Harbour, Valletta is also host to a Good Friday procession. Altar boys participate in the event in their traditional outfits.

overleaf: The city of Valletta gives the impression of floating on the seas that surround it.

An aerial view of Valletta which clearly illustrates its strategic position between the Grand and Marsamxett Harbours. From its fortifications defenders could dominate the entrances to both these harbours.

A site that has welcomed many a mariner entering the Grand Harbour.

A stretch of warehouses situated behind the fish market on Barriera Wharf. The wharf took its name from the barriers that were once present in this areas. These barriers controlled the arriving passengers as they made their way to clear quarantine.

The *Nix Mangiare* steps, so-called after the beggars' call for alms as sailors walked up to the city for shore leave.

Pinto's Stores: Grand Master Pinto was a Portuguese nobleman who was Grand Master of the Order of the Knights of St John from 1741–73. He completed crucial building work on the Auberge de Castille – now the offices of the Prime Minister of Malta – and erected these nineteen stores on the Valletta waterfront near Floriana. Pinto himself was an unpopular Grand Master, having upset some established noble families on the island by creating new noble titles and also by imposing heavy taxes. His legacy, though, is an important architectural one for Valletta.

The Waterfront area has been restored and a regeneration process has begun. Now the trade is very different and consists mainly of massive cruise liners carrying visitors to the island.

Despite the bombing onslaught of the Luftwaffe in World War II the city remained surprisingly intact, preserving its unique character made up of various architectural layers from a number of historical periods.

Valletta's fish market comes alive in the early hours of the morning when local fishermen converge to offload their catch.

overleaf: In the past crowds gathered on the fortifications to watch the return of the Mediterranean fleet. Today, people use the same vantage points to follow the start of the Annual Rolex Middle Sea Race as it departs on a gruelling 606 nautical mile course around Sicily and its islands.

A modern photographic rendition of the bird's eye views of the Grand Harbour so popular with eighteenth century engravers.

Fishermen use the traditional *frejgatina* for fishing inside harbour waters or just offshore.

9 Fort St Elmo

The walls of Fort St Elmo present a powerful image from the sea. Those approaching from the sea were left with little doubt as to the threat posed by the surrounding walls and guns.

Maritime architecture at its best where sea, wall and rock combine into a formidable defensive structure.

The lower sections of the fortifications throughout the Grand Harbour are carved down to the bedrock. Subsequently the stone quarried from these ditches would be used to build the upper part of the fortifications. The Knights of the Order of St John saw the value of this harbour complex and set about making it an impregnable fortress.

overleaf: Man-made structures around the Grand Harbour were built to withstand the tests of time. North easterly storms (*gregale*) batter the Grand Harbour area between the months of October and April.

195

Abercrombie Curtain: the curtain wall at St Elmo was first built in the 1680s and the casemated battery on top of the wall added by the British in the nineteenth century. This allowed cannon to fire right across the harbour if necessary. Halfway along the wall at the base there is 'sally point' (now blocked) from which knights and other soldiers could engage enemies in hand-to-hand fighting.

The layers of Valletta's history are clearly visible. Architecture from various phases of Malta's history sit comfortably alongside each other. The metal structure on the right replaced the historic stone lighthouse built by the Knights.

The Abercrombie Bastion is a key part of the defences of St Elmo at the entrance to the Grand Harbour. It is named after one of Britain's foremost military commanders of the eighteenth century, Sir Ralph Abercrombie. Although he had little to do with Malta he fought a decisive battle against the French in Egypt and he was brought to the naval hospital in Malta after being wounded in Alexandria, only to die there. He is buried in the walls of the bastion.

The ditch in front of Abercrombie Bastion is carved out of the rock, with the excavated stone used as building material for the fortifications and general building work. The bastion shown at the end flank is Alexander Ball bastion named after the first British governor. Ball was the commander of HMS Alexander and had fought with Nelson at the Battle of the Nile. He, more than anyone, ensured that after the French had been driven from Malta, the island became an English Protectorate. Ball, like Abercrombie, is buried within the bastion walls on the upper part of Fort St Elmo.

Lower St Elmo with the St Gregory bastion to the right. In the middle of the bastion, set into the lower fortifications, there is a patched-up stretch of wall where there was once a searchlight emplacement. These were important devices for guarding against any seaborne attack at night. From this close to the water, searchlights could be shone both across the harbour and into the water. Throughout World War II, these were used to check for U-boats and invading frogmen.

Straight streets form part of the grid plan
conceived for the city of Valletta by
its designer, the great Italian architect
Francesco Laparelli.

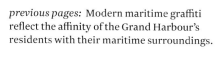
previous pages: Modern maritime graffiti reflect the affinity of the Grand Harbour's residents with their maritime surroundings.

A staggering perspective that highlights the sheer immensity of the Grand Harbour's fortifications.

Throughout the history of the Grand Harbour it was deemed essential to use physical barriers as an additional means of defending the harbour from seaborne attacks. During the Knights' period, a heavy metal chain was strung across the harbour mouth (at a height of about a metre above the level of the sea) to prevent ships from entering the main harbour areas. With the advent of submarines in the twentieth century, engineers had to deal with the threat of an underwater attack. In addition to the searchlights they also constructed an underwater curtain made of steel mesh, that stretched from St Elmo across the harbour – the Boom Defence. It was their solution to the threat of submarine and torpedo attacks and it proved devastatingly effective. On the morning of 26th July 1941 the Italians launched an E-boat attack on the harbour. The plan was to break through the curtain and subsequently, once they had done so, the intention was for 17 E-boats to attack the British vessels berthed in the Grand Harbour.

However it all went very wrong; the fleet was detected after a massive explosion by the Breakwater bridge, which fell and prevented the execution of the original plan. The remaining E-boats and 'human torpedoes' were wiped out by the guns at St Elmo and Fort Ricasoli, ably commanded by Colonel H. Frendo.

The control centre of the Boom Defence.
The memorabilia on the wall here commem-
orate the exploits of the navy and soldiers
World War II.

HAWSER
ANCHORAGE
ABUTMENT
1905

HAWSER: A LARGE ROPE FOR TOWING,
MOORING, OR SECURING A
SHIP

ANCHORAGE: A PLACE WHERE VESSELS
ANCHOR; A PLACE
SUITABLE FOR
ANCHORING

ABUTMENT: THE PLACE AT WHICH
ABUTTING OCCURS

Fort Ricasoli seen from inside the control
centre of the Boom Defence.

overleaf: Reaching out into the open sea
from whence the wild north-easterlies blow.